MW00779790

A Love Letter to You

STEPHAN LABOSSIERE
& C.J. ANTHONY

Copyright

A Love Letter to You

Copyright ©2023 by Stephan Labossiere for Stephan Speaks, LLC
Published by Highly Favored Publishing
First Edition: October 2023

All rights reserved. No part of this book may be used or reproduced in any manner whatsoever without written permission except in the case of brief quotations embodied in critical articles or reviews.

For more information, contact Highly Favored Publishing –
highlyfavoredent@gmail.com

Unless otherwise indicated, all scripture quotations are taken from the Holy Bible, New Living Translation, copyright © 1996, 2004, 2015 by Tyndale House Foundation. Used by permission of Tyndale House Publishers, Inc., Carol Stream, Illinois 60188. All rights reserved.

Scripture quotations marked MSG are taken from *The Message*, copyright © 1993, 2002, 2018 by Eugene H. Peterson. Used by permission of NavPress. All rights reserved. Represented by Tyndale House Publishers.

Editor & Creative Consultant: C. Nzingha Smith, SNC2 INK, LLC
Book Interior: A Darned Good Book – www.adarnedgoodbook.com
Images: Bianca Van Dijk for Pixaby stock photographs & images.

ISBN No. 978-1-957955-04-9

PRINTED AND BOUND IN THE UNITED STATES OF AMERICA

Dedication

This book is dedicated to women everywhere because every woman genuinely deserves to be showered with unconditional love.

It's dedicated to every woman I've met along my life's path, who has helped shape both my personal and professional journeys. Thinking of you brought me so much inspiration.

Even though no two women are the same, I used threads of truth most common for women with the intention to express love to each individual as well as the collective.

Table of Contents

Introduction

Dear, Love.

I wrote, *A Love Letter to You,* as a way to shower you with all the words you deserve to hear as someone who is deeply loved and who deserves to be celebrated just for who you are as a woman.

The entire book is intended to be read as one long love letter to you. It's meant to pour words of adoration, encouragement, and positivity into you. I want my words and voice to whisper in your ear and rekindle the sparks that might have since died out over time, but that can be revived by love's creative intent.

I pray as you read the love notes and poetry, they will touch your heart in a way that allows you to be open to receive this type of praise and adoration as the new "norm."

I pray this book will help you to voluntarily break down every barrier you've built in and around your heart in the name of "protection." The barriers meant to protect you, may act as a block, keeping you and your heart closed off from what God wants you to have, to be, and to experience.

Remember that all things are possible for those who believe. I want to rekindle in you the belief in the unlimited possibilities of experiencing love in its purest form. I also want to help you reconnect with your truest essence, unconditional love, and acceptance for Self just as you are in this now moment.

You are enough.

Scripture

"So, this is my prayer: that your love will flourish and that you will not only love much but well. Learn to love appropriately. You need to use your head and test your feelings so that your love is sincere and intelligent, not sentimental gush. Live a lover's life, circumspect and exemplary, a life Jesus will be proud of: bountiful in fruits from the soul, making Jesus Christ attractive to all, getting everyone involved in the glory and praise of God."
Philippians 1:9-11 MSG

Loving Your Feminine + Intuitive Being

Dear, Love.

When I think of what femininity is for a woman, it's literally just you being you. You being your true Self. Not what you think you should be, not what pride leads you to pretend to be, and not what fear holds you back from being.

But how your heart truly leads you to show up in the world. What your peace leads you to say. How your happiness leads you to interact with others and you being confident in that. No. Matter. What.

Au Natural

Femininity
more than just a behavioral trait
it resides deep within
you, woman.

It's home,
coded in your DNA
present in the structure
of your very Being
God's organic design for
you, woman.

Traits selected
specific to who you were
to be, naturally
it's how He internally wired
you, woman.

Somehow, (maybe) you
have been torn away from
or even in some respects,
shamed away
from embracing yourself
as whole, more than
the sum total
of all your parts.

Leading you to operate
out of alignment
with whom you really are,
Divine Feminine.

Super Energy

Sexy
inebriating
alluring
tender
but not weak,

powerful
in its ability to command
and get what it wants
not pushy or tough,

sensual
because of its softness
more powerful
than physical force,
a true man's weakness,

influential in creating
peace and harmony
and outcomes of cooperation
if used for good
the super energy
woman's femininity.

Dear, Love.

You were supplied with everything you need to accomplish your purpose here on Earth during the time you're given. I want you to see yourself as capable and well-equipped.

When you have faith and unshakable belief in yourself, you will be unstoppable.

Right Order

Admire
appreciate
adore
you, first
must be the beholder,
your own adoration
and self-love
the key,

to unlocking infinite
limitless
possibilities of love
flow through you,
your reservoirs
never empty,
dry or lacking
tap in.

Honest Existence

Trying to squeeze
into other's perceptions
no longer fits,
(all) labels
you've since outgrown.

Living from outdated versions
false projections
no longer suit you,
no need for self-judgement
there's nothing wrong
with you.

Fundamentally
you're right, in every way
simply being
a state of honest existence,
live out of your essence
the best way you know how
honor your truth.

Dear, Love.

Everything about you is perfection because God made you masterfully.

Once you begin to live from this truth, you automatically repel the low vibrational energy that would get you tangled up with toxic dysfunction in relationships for good.

Of course, this also means that even people you love and care about might need to be included in the "best left behind" category.

Trust it's for your own highest good. There's better in store, including not needing to shrink or dim your light for the benefit or comfort of others. Be you, unapologetically.

Ascend

Building new foundations
requires
letting go.

Time to ascend.

The material
you've worked with
previously,
is no longer needed.

Time to ascend.

Self-imposed barriers
used as a means to protect
now hold you down (captive)
and longing to express
your truth (love) freely.

Time to ascend.

Knowing

Intuitively knowing
rely solely on your
faith
to carry you through

a breakthrough
of awareness is all
you really need.

Re-Member You

Go within,
observe what's seen
fall in love
with the you,
you really are
acceptance, the elixir
essential nourishment.

Supernatural wonder
picturesque beauty,
royal,
eternal light in focus,
needed, always
sufficient.

Brings a revelation
of whose you are
a vital member of God's
body, chosen, set apart
precious, honored
loved, protected.

Truth reconnects you
with your innate abilities,
able to see way
beyond the surface of
what's normally perceived
heightened intuition
among your many amazing
superpowers, a superb,
super Being.

Dear, Love.

Everything that has happened to you up until this point has helped sharpen and refine the tools you were Divinely entrusted with to assist you on your unique journey.

Each experience was purposed to build you up and equip you, not tear you down or destroy you. Everything works together for the good of those who love God. Trust God's plan.

Using this point of view as a filter will help you gain awareness from everything that comes your way going forward so you can get the needed lessons and integrate them in real time.

A Choice

Life giver
you're everything and more
no need to shrink
or compete,
you've already won.

Somewhere
you lost confidence
in the Being God made
you to be, feeling
insignificant and/or out of place
the real you forgotten.

Comfortable playing a "role"
pacifying your real needs
disregarding your
bona fide essence
a choice.

Choose differently, now,
believe you're enough
at your most beautiful
operating in
your own
authenticity.

Reflections

Feminine energy
a massive emotional range
varied in beauty and
complexity,

deceptive terrain
to roaming eyes
they settle for the mirage
missing the powerful,

nourishing
qualities you possess
just below the surface,
reflections.

Dear, Love.

Your feminine energy is free flowing. It doesn't need structure nor does it need to be restrained in the rigid confines of logic or outdated tradition.

It needs the flexibility to fill up space, to pour positivity and love into the hollow places of all of life's voids.

In Tact

Life,
failed love,
disappointments
and heartbreak
didn't break you
you're still in tact
different,
changed maybe
but not broken, just in need
of some loving attention,
a proper tending to.

Weightless

Endless possibilities
await you...

[voluntarily allow
the heaviness,
bitterness, mistrust,
baggage of the past,
anger, and defensiveness
to fall away]

...once weightless.

Dear, Love.

Who lied to you and told you that you're supposed to be hard, tough, bitter, guarded, emotionally unattached and unavailable?

More importantly, why did you believe them?

It's time to get back in touch with and operate aligned with God's design for you. Begin to take steps to reconnect with your Divine Feminine Energy if you've lost touch.

Start by listening to yourself, learning to trust your instincts, and following through on your intuitive guidance. It's always patiently present and waiting for you to access it for your good.

Presence

Presence in the present
a gift, a new time of
seeing yourself again
for the first time
with rejuvenated eyes,
full of restored compassion.

Past falls
caused you to doubt
yourself,
opt for forgiveness,
decide now to be present.

Presence in the present
an offering, a new time of
welcoming in tolerance
patient kindness,
total acceptance
for you as you are
in this moment.

Consciously remaining in
the period of time
occurring now,
the present,
disarms the past,
well done
you made it
you can now move on.

Vision

Way beyond
a surface
knowing

you hold
instinctively
deeper truths

when in tune and aligned,
with the Creator's
vision for you.

Go Within

Mysterious
you are the magic
and the magical
forever able to bring
forth
more brilliance and
light
all you seek
you'll find
you are,
go within.

Dear, Love.

Listen to yourself. This will help you to start to trust yourself again. Get reacquainted with who you truly are. It's vital for you to follow your own intuition and inner guidance. Doing so is a natural confidence booster. It's also one of your most important superpowers and connects you directly to your Divinity.

Harmonious

Ruled by feelings,
emotive and sensing
there's a natural
connectedness
you possess,
your femininity entwines
you with everything
effortlessly,
when embracing her,
your natural vibration
emits harmony, with
life in all its many
forms.

Approval

Your *true* Self
yearns for your
unconditional
approval.

Dear, Love.

Your relationship with yourself sets the tone for all the other relationships you'll have in life. External things are limited. You, my dear, are not.

Don't go looking for reflections of yourself in others before you have built a solid foundation of who you are based on God's word, self-acceptance, and unconditional love for Self.

Sure, others can help you learn things about yourself and can assist you with your own self-discovery, but they can also get you off track and cause you to lose all or parts of yourself, which will serve and benefit them and not you.

Creating a solid foundation rooted in self-love and acceptance will help you know your worth and value it no matter what.

Healer

Realigning with your original
ways of Being,
once understood
begin to mend discord within,
the duality
your humanness + Divine essence
no longer at odds
initiates healing.

A process, cyclical in nature
never quite complete
reoccurring themes
make you think
no progress is being made.

But wait, you're changing,
growing
evolution is ensuing
even if you can't see
any evidence, stay the course.

The real change is happening
deep within,
similar to Chinese bamboo
progress is hidden
veiled underneath
darkness, dirt
protects from outside
unwanted tampering.

Realignment requires patience
right timing
consistent effort.

Once ready
major breakthrough
happens, you reemerge
stable, flexible
possessing strong
roots
able to create
offshoots
your healing energy
spreads,
contagion.

The overflow inspires,
grants permission and
access *to all*,
now an example
of what's possible
your choice to say yes
to realigning,
to be open,
to persist,
to heal,
heals.

Dear, Love.

You always know what's best. Relearn how to trust yourself by using (honoring) and (listening) to your intuitive voice and the Divine guidance (instincts) you've been entrusted with access to.

True Confidence

True confidence
pours out
from your feminine
energy
more specifically,
your femininity
its nurturing nature
brings out your
exceptionally
loving Spirit.

At your highest
expression,
there's a lightness
in your step
your Spirit is happy,
bubbly, refreshed,
able to be featherlike
in this state
of being
you're the most
desirable.

Dear, Love.

Spending time with yourself should be a welcomed habit.

Pray, ask yourself questions, talk to your Spirit and Soul. Get to know the inner workings of your Being. Get familiar with how your inner voice sounds.

What you'll discover is that what you need, or feel is missing in your life, is already within you and eager for you to rediscover its presence and put it to use.

You have to go within. You have a wealth of treasure in you waiting to be found, appreciated, and loved!

Come Forth

The fullness of your
potential
is urging you,
grant it permission
to come forth
arise and expand
into the fully realized
version
of the you,
you need to be now
say yes to her,
say no to continuing to
play small.

Dear, Love.

Thank you. Please forgive them and you. I love you. You matter. You are appreciated.

I stand in the gap for everyone in your life who didn't have the capacity or awareness to say these five short yet powerful statements to you throughout your life's journey.

Loving Your Heart

+ Emotions

Dear, Love.

You are safe. You are protected. You are valued. You are loved first and foremost by God, always.

God's love for you is unconditional and not based or measured by anything you do, your level of success, or any material possessions you're striving to obtain. You can't earn it.

God's love alone is enough to fill any and all voids within you. Every other type of loving relationship is possible from this sacred foundation.

Love is meant to be given freely and without conditions including the love you have for yourself. Connect to and build from love in its original intent, God's agape love.

Grace

Previous heartbreak
left your heart
fragmented
in a thousand pieces
changed parts
of you,

allow God to reframe
the picture
with the remnants
of what's left
a mosaic formed
fresh perspective,
deconstructed parts
repurposed,

held together
something new
created
only by the grace of
God
your indestructible
glue.

Re-member You

The heart of you
hasn't forgotten
tenderness
natural traits
weaponized
to the point of
self-hatred,

but Love, it's time
to create a new vision
piece by patient piece
of what you want to see
a reflection
staring back at you
of wholeness
re-member you.

Whole

You're not broken
sure, there are things
that caused you
at times to forget
to honor you,

to break down,
momentarily
to hurt
to cry
but not break,

you're still
intact
complete
whole.

Dear, Love.

You possess the kind of love that mends and protects. It consoles and heals. It cares for and nurtures. It's the kind of love that is pure and intense and authentic. It builds and supports. It's tender and sacred.

The love of your dreams is present, walking with you all the time. The special love you so freely give to other people, please recognize, value, and internalize it, so you too can reap its many benefits.

It's your love, after all. It belongs to you. It's not selfish to indulge in it at all times. Save some for you.

A Re-Introduction

Excuse me Miss
I mean no offense
to your heart.

Just to hear the sweet
sound of your voice
I'd honestly go by any name.

I am pure
something unlike
everything else you've
experienced.

If you don't mind
I'd just like to have a moment
in time to compliment
you on your one-of-a-kind
Self.

Let's get reacquainted
I've always been with you
residing in the depths, hidden,
I'm the *love* you're in wait of.

We've met on occasion
years passed, we lost touch
living from your heart
helps you find me again
and again, I belong to you,
I'm your love.

Heart-Centered

Flawlessly executed
rare beauty
personified
heart-centered
no need to compromise
your worth
or settle for
playing a role
of a lesser-than
version of the
extraordinary
original intended
one.

Acceptance

Accept
who you aren't
so the true you
can emerge
and come forth
perceptive to
experience
the miracles
accessible
in every moment
is possible for
you.

Open Heart

You're stardust
supplying
the sun
moon
galaxies
with needed
sparkle.

Radiant star,
your open heart
a fixed
luminous point,
shining bright
true north
lights the path
for others to follow.

Dear, Love.

Your experiences added character, resilience, and strength among other things to you. Think of them as the building material that only helped fortify you from the inside out. They were used and needed to mold and shape you, creating your profound uniqueness.

Sowing Seeds

Your unique love
expression is
powerful seed
salve and mender
therapy
enduring
everlasting
necessary.

By planting
your personal seeds
of love, in your heart's
fertile garden,
you create
even more love.

Increase

Mutual agreement
multiplies
anything liberally
including choosing
to love you.

Thank you for deciding.

A decision
you are meant
to continue
to make every day
that you wake up in spite
of any momentary
contrary feelings.

Once unconditional
love
develops
it will only continue
to increase
expand
throughout lifetimes
helping to nurture
future generations
to come
leaving behind
true legacy.

Dear, Love.

Your own love-filled words have power. They are keys. Be sure to use them to unlock unconditional love, positivity, and blessings into your life on a daily basis.

Sacred Conversations

Connected
in constant conversation
with the Creator
allows the veil
of the Spirit world
to lift
causes you to remember,
honor
follow
your heart's
sacred whispers.

Heart Whisperings

Drop into your heart
linger there
listen patiently,
it speaks
in soft whispers,
of long-since
muffled
desires.

Drop into your heart
see what secrets
it wants to tell,
feel the dreams
and yearnings
still stirring within you
wanting to be
brought to life
through you.

Drop into your heart
find out its deeper
callings
honor them
they will guide you
to total fulfillment
and abundance.

Your Nature

It's in your nature
to feel,

empathy
compassion
sensitivity
pleasure
pure joy
et al,

the sheer input
from your senses

fall back
in love
with the power
of your nature.

Dear, Love.

Start to celebrate and embrace all of your journey and the many sides of you in your entirety, including your whole heart and all of your emotions.

There's no need to discount or discard the shadow parts of you. They're valuable too. Everything about you is beautiful and sacred, making up the total vision of you.

Your emotions aren't meant to be things that you become ashamed of or try to hide. They are your guides and a part of the complete, bigger picture. You're in charge of the narrative. *No one else.*

Shadow Parts

Embracing
accepting
the dark
shadow parts
of you
means you're able
to fully
appreciate,
experience
your own light
it's natural,
it's beautiful
because it's a part
of *you*,
all of you existing
together
harmoniously
out of hiding.

Freedom

Love wills
and enables you
free yourself
from wrestling
duality
imbalance that originates
from forgetting
your true nature,

instead, realign
yourself to truth
connect
to your abundant
nature,
not lacking anything
health, wealth, happiness
flowing in
flowing out
overflowing
from you
enabling true
freedom.

Recognition

Raw emotions
in desperate
need of sincere
recognition
acknowledge your
feelings,
be attentive,
allow them room
to reveal deeper
wisdom, you are more
than flesh and blood.

Be willing to feel
it is safe and vital
live in harmony
with your heart's
truth,
its role
to assist and guide
you.

Recognition
comforts
soothes
brings peace within
facilitates
harmony
without.

Sacred Softness

Standing
in full acceptance
of your heart's
revelations
helps to recapture
childlike abandon
silly giggles
for no reason,

light you up
an inner glow so
radiant
a sacred softness
delicate, yet secure
seeking to be nurtured
regularly
gravitate back to
your heart center.

Dear, Love.

Constantly gift yourself tenderness and gentle patience as you journey on and navigate your unique life's path.

You also need to give yourself the gift of your own understanding and your own kindness. These are gifts you can use to shower yourself with on a daily basis.

Keep these gifts fully stocked so they're always at hand when you need to be nourished. No need to wait on others to do it for you. You have an ample amount of your own supply.

Awareness

There's a secret
admiration
often unexpressed
openly
by men for your
abilities

for your strength
for your resilience
for the mystery behind
a creation
so sensitive
and at the same time
resilient

you're used
to getting flack
about having to carry
the world on your
shoulders

what's not focused on
is your ability to do
just that
and then some.

Dear, Love.

There's no need to search outside of yourself for love, affection, security, knowledge, and approval.

You came fully equipped and capable of supplying yourself with everything you need.

All these things and more are in you for you. You possess them.

Feel

Don't let misplaced
judgement,
mock or poison
your ability to FEEL
deeply.

Depth
another
characteristic
synonymous
with woman.

Be willing to
brave the breadth
of your
vast
inner currents.

Trust
in the safety of
your sensitivity
often disguised
as anger or being
aloof.

Wisdom

Seek
and you will find
ask
and it will be given
to you,

proper discernment
knowledge
insight
revelation
the truth,

fully knowing
yourself
the highest form of
wisdom
and the hidden path
to loving yourself
completely.

I apologize, I didn't know.
I never meant to hurt you.

Please forgive me.
I love you.

Dear, Love.

How many times have you waited ever so patiently or longed for someone else to say these four phrases to you?

Maybe the words never came and because of that you've lingered and remained in your hurt.

Perhaps these are words you need to say to yourself for actions taken or perceived "mistakes" made.

Bless yourself now by telling you all the things you long to hear as often as needed.

Love you.

Self-Forgiveness

Written to be read as if you wrote it.

Please forgive me.
I didn't know
what I was going
through at the time
culture told me
it wasn't cool,
to show vulnerability
was weakness,
to ask for help,
to admit I was hurting.

Please forgive me.
I didn't know
which way to go,
I didn't know
I was destroying you
in the process
of hiding my pain.

Please forgive me.
I'm working to
come back to you
a little more every day,
I still have no clue
but with every honest
admission,
I gain a little
more clarity.

Please love me as I am.
I am doing my best,
it's enough.

I forgive you.
You are safe with me.
I'll never abandon you.
I love you.
Love, Me.

Loving Your
Human Nature

Dear, Love.

Choose to measure yourself by God's standards alone. Spend adequate time in the presence of God so that He can show you the original design for your life and how He created you for His glory and purpose.

Gratitude

The birther and
sustainer of life
and everything
precious,

the words formed here
can't accurately
express
tell
articulate

the heartfelt
gratitude
reverence
respect
felt for

the magnitude
that is, you,
in all your
necessary
metamorphosis
past, present, future.

Human

To be human is
to make mistakes
to move
at your own pace,
to *not need* to be
perfect
to not measure yourself
according to outside
standards.

To be human is
to need self-compassion
to need patience for   inconsistent
growth patterns
and a steady stream of
self-forgiveness.

To be human is
to not have to know it all,
to be unique
and true to Self
to not be defined by
anyone else
or their expectations
is to be human.

Natural Rights

Being human
is your natural right,
no outside permission
required
release restraint
permit
allow
the proper space
and grace
needed
for you
are a human, being
yourself,
that's enough.

Dear, Love.

You were created to stand out. Not in an awkward way, but in a way that would complement those you keep company with because you embrace who you are, authentically.

Stop worrying about fitting in. It's not possible. You were created to be unique and dynamic.

Seen

Embrace the vast
essence of your true
embodiment
both the tangible
obvious expressions
in addition to the hidden
parts, you've wanted to ignore,
nothing is for nothing
it all matters
give all of you room
to be fully seen.

Fullness

Totality
beginning and end
it's in your nature
to take up space
you belong here,

to be allowed to exist
spread out and still whole
in the entirety of
your uninhibited
fullness.

Dear, Love.

You are adequate. You are desirable. You are prized. The inability or decision of other people to not value you is not a measure of your true worth. It's a choice they made. Nothing more.

Misfit

Misappropriated
standards
the opposite of
your truth
don't fit
the misfit, a rebel
you're not meant to
conform
into others' realities.

To see yourself
as you really are
and ought to be
gives you the
freedom
liberation from
playing a role.

Too many masks
covering up,
smothering,
suffocating
your actual
unlimited
potential.

Breathe

Pause
stop for a second
simply, take a slow
inhale in, hold it,
exhale slowly
breathe deeply.

Relax
you are exactly
where you ought
to be
in this present
moment.

Unlearning,
forgetting
re-learning
discovering
new things,
safe.

Dear, Love.

Begin to practice being yourself based on God's version of who He created you to be. Operate from this place on a daily basis. Base your self-perception on God's design for you and not a distorted worldly "less-than" version.

It's not about needing to change who you are, but the way you're choosing to see yourself and the place you're operating from. Because you're going to be what you practice being regularly.

Phases

You are
and will always be
forever changing,
evolving,
reinventing,
becoming
better
stronger
more yourself
more realized.

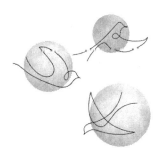

Reimagine

Re-imagine a flexible
agile
dynamic existence,
at peace
with and within
yourself
in life
in love
in relationships,

reconnecting to
your nature
free will
a choice
allows
autonomy
fluidity
the flowing
of such existence

your new vision
supports
manifestation
first, within you
with the excess
spilling abundantly
over into
every other area
of your life.

Dear, Love.

I love how you manage to make being so many things look so effortless, it's pure magic to witness. The numerous roles you play and all the many titles a woman has in life are constantly changing and you master them with ease.

Discovery

Magnificent (magnificence)
lies hidden
an outward quality
harnessed by few
envied by many
solely witnessed by the
discerning,

can only be produced,
fashioned
created
from that which resides
within you,

a multitude of depth
raw materials
forgotten
devalued, lie hidden
waiting to be
(re)discovered.

The Gift of You

No special occasion needed
you are the Gift.

A finished work,
the whole dream of you
manifested
a masterpiece.

An act of God's
loving genius.

The Mirage

Realizing
who you are
beyond the human form
gives you access to
your Divinity,

a Spirit being
(way more than perceived flesh)
having a human experience
in this space and time

distraction causes you
to disconnect from truth
and purpose
believing in what's
not actually real

illusion
leaves you
perpetually
unfulfilled

don't settle
stay persistent
in pursuit
of your truth
a vital step
to forgo the
mirage.

Dear, Love.

To believe in yourself and your worth is to reclaim your power. This allows the weight of guilt, shame, fear of rejection, and victimhood mentality to fall away. You are all that is necessary and sufficient. You're not just your physical body though, you're so much more.

Balancing Acts

Flexibility (adaptability)
is your strength
the capacity (power)
to backbend (bend backwards)
without breaking
you, my dear
are a force.

Dear, Love.

After all you've been through, survived, overcome, it's time to gift yourself the peace you so truly deserve. It's not something that comes from anything external. It comes from within. It's a decision you make and stay committed to every single day, no matter what.

Loving Your
Body + Mind

Dear, Love.

You are smoothness and elegance of movement. You embody poise, charm, flow, ease, and Divine grace.

You have the spontaneous, unmerited gift of Divine favor as a covering over you. You have Divine influence operating in all areas of your life, daily.

You are highly regarded with favor. You are the most remarkable creature ever created. Hands down.

Embodied Grace

Poised
elegant
charming
the epitome of God's
grace,
woman.

Soften

Originally soft to the touch
so filled with love
skin's elasticity
resilient,
but often stretched
too thin, beyond its limits

creates changes
to the outside structure
a shell forms,
thick-skinned
protective barriers
hide your natural sensitivity
and desire to live out a
soft existence

makes it hard
to feel you out,
and know your needs
now defensive,
yet still in need of connection
a sense of safety within
will allow you, to shed the thick
rough, hardened skin,
I urge you, please,
soften again.

Synonyms

Soft and woman are
synonymous,
one in the same,
neither of which is
weak.

Dear, Love.

Fall in love with the way God made you. It's crucial for you to be your own body-positive support system for all things uplifting to your Spirit about the way you look, how your body is shaped, be it your freckles, hair type, your beautiful mind, and the list goes on.

More often than not, we look for outside validation from others because secretly it's our own validation we crave. It's our own approval; we wish we had the courage to gift ourselves.

Well, my dear, it begins and ends with accepting everything about you and ultimately choosing to love the way you were created, down to the cellular level and every level in-between.

Breathtaking

The skies opened up
down you came
passing me by,

I managed to soak up
your scent
the sweet aroma of
euphoria mixed
with the after scent of
heaven,

engulfed my senses,
got caught up in my lungs
losing my breath
your Spirit Being,
manifested in physical
form,
breathtaking.

Your Physical

Curvy or slim fine
where do I begin,
to describe
all the different kinds
of exquisite you
personify,

defying time
ageless
flawless
beauty,

sexiness
drips easily from every
inch of your body
pools, spilling forth

displaying
varying degrees of your
remarkable appeal
your physical,
intoxicating
addictive.

Skin

Perfect in your own
skin
allow yourself
room
to glow up
alter shape,

just as the seasons
change
you'll need space
to do the same
embrace it,

take care to
protect and appreciate
your outermost
multidimensional
layer.

Light

God cast you
from the sun
so, I know you are
one of a kind
I see you both
share
produce
yield
the same rays of light
sometimes hidden
but always present
beyond any temporary
cloudiness.

Dear, Love.

Your full spectrum authentic Self is the most beautiful sight to see, ever. Never shy away from showing off and flaunting it. There's something really special about being able to experience the full, radiant view of you in all your vibrant splendor, straight up, no chaser.

Sacred

Originating from
an inner wisdom
ancient and sacred
a source of love that comes
from deep within

sparks a happiness,
a confidence
that spreads warmth to
and from your heart,

brings a sparkle to
your eyes
a delighted,
captivating smile
rests upon your lips.

Smile

Your smile
holds enough wattage
to light up even the darkest
of nights

a sight more profound
transforming
healing
disarming

the exact opposite of
cultural norm's
resting b*@#! face

be a rebel
be alive
be joy-filled
show off
your radiant,
much-needed smile.

Speechless

What more can I say?
A glimpse of your aura
blinds, temporarily
overwhelms.

The hue of matte red
laid perfectly
upon your lips
seduces.

I appreciate
the care you take,
the details matter.

Dear, Love.

Appreciate who you are in this moment, just as you are. You are so special, so dope, so rare.

Any improvements, additions, or upgrades you wish to make to your mind or body don't change the fact that right now, at this point in time, you are still a site to behold, to admire, to praise.

You are a perfectly crafted model of uniquely fashioned beauty.

Show acceptance for yourself and love you throughout your many physical and mental transformations, both large and small.

Being you is always enough. Showing up as yourself with no filter is when you are most desirable.

Standout

You don't fit
a particular category
or the popular image
even though
every *other* secretly
emulates
imitation, the greatest
form of flattery,
what comes naturally
for you.

The Shapes You Take

Integrity intact
faultless and resolute
unspoken...weight
of burdens lifted.

Light illuminates from the
fullness
that is your silhouette
striking and electric.

Aura captivates, intimidates
arouses all the senses
awakened to your presence
substance spilling over,
overwhelming
to witness
the many shapes
you take.

Shape Shifter

Shape changes with a
shift in your step
shadows dance
just to get closer to
you.

A brush up against
your essence thrills,
a soft-spoken word, woos
the images you create
in observing minds
will never be
erased.

Permanently
engrained
closed eyes can
still see
your endless
ever-changing
shapes shifting.

Behold

An old adage says
beauty is in the eyes
of the beholder.

Let me behold you.

My eyes roam
pleased
at what they see
perpetual
exquisite
captivating
spectacular you.

Dear, Love.

Beauty is not just seen with the eyes but witnessed with the entire being. It's a multi-sensory experience. Thank you for allowing us to bear witness to the breadth of you.

Beautiful

Beautiful
a simple word
in its attempt to
summarize the
attributes that make up
you.

An adjective meant to
describe traits
of excellence attached
to physical qualities
generally pleasing
to the eyes and senses.

So beautiful,
goes a step further
to emphasize adoration
roaming eyes could sit and gaze
drowning in the wonder
your aesthetic produces
always.

Dear, Love.

Possessing a beautiful mind is just as important to the overall appeal you possess as your physical attractiveness is.

Beautiful minds recognize and respect each other. The mind has a powerful way of attracting things that are in harmony with it, good and bad. Being smart, intelligent, caring, confident, humorous, kind, independent, and supportive stems from your having a beautiful mind to compliment and make up the full package.

Always strive to continue to stretch and develop your mental muscles the same way you work your body out regularly to stay in shape.

Brilliant Mind

Intellectual
mysterious
strategic
creative
stretching perceived
mental limitations
connecting beyond
physical and emotional
levels up
your ability to
intimately
relate
link
tap in
with other
brilliant minds.

Quick Wit

Razor sharp
perceptive
discerning
your ability
to never not know
how to respond to
external
stimuli
on point
rebuttal
creates intrigue
makes you stand out
memorable
for your quick wit
the highest form
of intellectual prowess.

Dear, Love.

Admiring and showering yourself with loving words and compliments dissolves negative, self-defeating inner talk.

It's time to switch out your default inner voice of self-criticism with a more loving inner voice filled with self-admiration.

When you're admiring yourself, you automatically show yourself love and produce the highest frequency of self-love and acceptance.

Loving yourself in this way allows you to vibrate higher, and become a magnet for the good meant for you to experience in every area of your life.

Set Apart

Ask any potential "matches"
one qualifying question:
Have you prayed for me?

If his answer is no.
Please note:
You are way out of his league.

You're too much of a prize
to become someone's
perhaps
or short-term obligation,
a good for now,
or a good enough.

You can't settle
being his compulsive decision,
a lukewarm fantasy,
or a flashy object he takes out
for special occasions
to show off to his friends and
colleagues.

While it might seem like flattery,
just leave yourself free
for the right someone
to come along

who has taken the time to
get to know you
in your Spirit Being.

He has been specific
as it pertains to the qualities
which make up you in your entirety.

Your love is what will be added
to compliment him,
and he will be the physical
representation
of God's love for you.

He will know your value
as a precious gift from God
to be protected and cherished,
always.

In the meantime,
excuse all the surface level
"matches"
who don't come prepared
or equipped to claim the prize.

Instead, spend time praying
for the *one* that's truly
meant for you.

Because the right "match"
your Boaz, will continuously
pray until he receives
that which his heart desires
to be delivered in God's
right timing
as a miracle specific to his
particular needs,

the type of woman
who is set apart,
his answer to a yet to be
answered prayer... *You.*

Closing Scripture

"[God] You are the one who created my innermost parts;
you knit me together while I was still in my mother's womb.
I give thanks to you that I was marvelously set apart.
Your works are wonderful—I know that very well."
Psalm 139:13-14

The End.

About the Author

Stephan Labossiere is *the* "Relationship Guy." An authority on real love, real talk, real relationships. The brand *Stephan Speaks* is synonymous with happier relationships and healthier people around the globe. For more than a decade, Stephan has committed himself to breaking down relationship barriers, pushing past common facades, and exposing the truth. It is his understanding of REAL relationships that has empowered millions of people, clients, and readers alike, to create their best lives by being able to experience and sustain greater love.

Seen, heard, and chronicled in national and international media outlets including, *The Tom Joyner Morning Show*, *The Examiner*, *ABC*, *GQ*, and *Huffington Post Live*. The certified life & relationship coach, speaker, and award winning, bestselling author is the voice that the world tunes into for answers to their difficult relationship woes. From understanding the opposite sex, to navigating the paths and avoiding the pitfalls of relationships and self-growth, Stephan's relationship advice and insight helps countless men and women overcome the situations hindering them from achieving an authentically amazing life.

"My message is simple: life and relationships require truth. The willingness to speak truth and the bravery to acknowledge truth is paramount." Are you listening? Enough said.

Other Books by Stephan Speaks

40 Prayers for My Future Husband,
Preparing to Receive the Marriage God Has for Me
www.prayersformyfuturehusband.com

The Man God Has for You
www.TheManGodHasForMe.com

Love After Heartbreak, Vol. 1
www.LoveAfterHeartbreak.com

Daily Affirmations for Healing
Love After Heartbreak, Vol. 1 Companion Book
www.AffirmationsForHealing.com

Healing Heartbreak Journal
Love After Heartbreak, Vol. 1 Companion Book
www.HealingHeartbreakBook.com

He's Lying Sis
www.HesLyingSis.com

God Where is My Boaz?
www.GodWhereIsMyBoaz.com

Prayers For My Marriage
www.PrayersForMyMarriageBook.com

Made in the USA
Las Vegas, NV
11 February 2025

17955704R00079